The Path To Peace: A Never Ending Struggle!

Gumaa Francis Lodongi

Table of Contents

Dedication

Dedicated to father South Sudan and mother Sudan (united).

I love you so very much! My Faithfuls and Admirers.

Acknowledgments

First of all, I want to say that I am very happy for this book to be my latest accomplishment. It is very exciting but also humbling to have written a book about an idea that we all take for granted, that is peace. It is an idea we also misunderstand. This book was inspired by the hopes and dreams of our beloved nation South Sudan and Sudan. And also from the countless struggles we faced as global citizens, yearning every day of our lives for that moment in which we will be present in the stillness that is peace.

First and foremost, as a token of gratitude, I want to thank my lovely mother, Asonta Odowa Ogeri, and father, Francis Loboy Ohiri, maternal and paternal grandparents, aunties and uncles, cousins, nieces and nephews, and overall my brothers and sisters. I also want to thank my teachers, coaches, women and men who have trained and taught me in academics so that I can be educated and turn out to be the humbly brilliant man I am today.

I am also thankful for my inspirational icons including President Barack Obama, Criss Angel, his holiness Pope Francis, David Blaine, David Copperfield, Michelle Obama, Emma Watson, Angelina Jolie, Oprah Winfrey, Michael Jordan, James Randi, Michael Cain, etc,. I also am very grateful once again to one of my mentors Criss Angel for his effortful contribution to my current success. I appreciate all the influences of President Salva Kiir Mayardit, Dr. Riek Machar, President Donald J. Trump, President Justin Trudeau, his highness Prince Charles, his highness Prince Phillip, and her majesty Queen Elizabeth II.

I also want to thank the former political ministers who applied their complete contribution to making South Sudan and Sudan the lovely nation it is today. These people are Abd al-Rahman Al Mahdi, Ismail al-Zhari, Abdallah Khalil, Ibrahim Abboud, Siir Al Khatim Al Khalifa, Muhammad Ahmad Mahgoub, Sadiq al-Mahdi, Babiker Awadalla, Jaafar Nimeiry, Rashid Bkr, al-Jazuli Daf'allah, Bakri Hassan Saleh, Motazz Moussa, Mohamed Tahir Ayala, Abdalla Hamdok, Omar Al-Bashir, Abdel Rahman Swar Al-Dahab.

I also express honorably my gratitude towards our fellow South Sudanese founders who also fought tirelessly and painfully to inspire the nation towards independence, peace, justice, liberty, and greater prosperity. This prosperity is growing more everyday, engaging the human hearts of our fellow South Sudanese and Sudanese people as one nation. These founders are Dr. John Garang, Salva Kiir Mayardit, Dr. Riek Machar, James Wani Igga, Taban Deng Gai, Rebecca Nyandeng Garang, Hussein Abdelbagi, Nhial Deng Nhial, Josephine Joseph Lagu, Onyoti Adagio Nyikec, Martin Elia Lomuro, Kuol Athian Mawien, Nadia Arop Dudi, Angelina Teny, John Luk Jok, Peter Marcallo Nasir,

Josephine Napwon Cosmas, Lasuba L. Wango, Athian Ding Athian, Beatrice Wani-Noah, Ayaa Benjamin Warille, Awut Deng, Achuil, Elizabeth Acuei Yor, Deny Jock Chagor, Michael Chanjiek Geay, Peter Mayen, Michael Makuei Lweth, Paul Mayom Akec, Manoah Peter Gatkuoth, Ruben Madol Aroi, James Hoth Mai, Henry Dilang Odwar, Obote Mamur Mete, Jemma Nunu Kumba, Stephen Par Kuol, Puok Kang Choi, Simon Mijok Majak, Madut Biar Yol, Rizik Zakaria Hassan, Mayiik Ayii Deng, James Janka Duku, Martin Elia Lomuro, Paul Mayom Akec, Dr. Nadia Arop Dudi, Gen. Kuol Manyan Juuk, Dr. Dhieu Mathok Diing, Josephine Napon, Salvatore Garang Mabiordit, Awut Deng Acuil, Deng Deng Hoc, Dr. Riak Gai Kok, Yen Oral Lam, Dr. Lado Gore, Hussein Mar Nyot, Michael Makue Loweth, Michael Chiengjiek, Sophia Pal Gai, Paulino Wanawilla, James Hoth Mai, Obote Mamur Mete , Peter Bashir Bande, Ezekiel Lul Gatkuoth, Rebecca Joshua Okwaci, John Luk Jok, and Jemma Nunu Kumba.

Last but not least, of course, my appreciation and gratitude are endless for all the wonderful and incredible Humanity that has helped, disciplined, edified, strengthened, and empowered me. That is all the women and men to who I will be forevermore indebted. May God bless all of you, my Faithfuls and Admirers! May God also bless father South Sudan and mother Sudan and all you wonderful readers who read this book and appreciate it, and those members of

iv

Humanity who reside in the entire rest of the global earth. Cheers!

About the Author

Gumaa Francis Lodongi was born and raised in the beautiful Kosti, Sudan, and immigrated to the beloved Canada to seek better opportunities. He wished to fulfill his dreams and goals of becoming a successful renaissance man by being an Actor, Model, Inventor, Entrepreneur, Humanitarian, Global Leader, Politician, and overall a showbiz entertainer with the inclination to break barriers, enliven matter, and Humanity. He has seen the likes of many renaissance men such as Leonardo da Vinci, David MichelAngelo accomplish incredible success and prosperity in multiple spheres. Gumaa Francis Lodongi aspires to do a similar thing, with the exception of a plot twist.

He has lived in Sudan until the age of 9 years old and for 18 years in Canada growing and learning through cultural and traditional assimilation so that he can live the Canadian dream and spice up the diversity of Canada through his own personal upbringing to engage the human heart and re-engage the human spirit.

In this book, he aims to redefine the purpose of immigration, Inhumanity, discrimination, stereotypes, etc. by attempting to instill hope, faith, and optimism in Humanity that they may have redemptive power to live an extraoardinary life, whether they're here in Canada, or somewhere else.

That is evolutionary progress as Gumaa likes to put it. No matter the racial, national, or religious background, you can have individualistic inner and outer peace. He wishes for his Faithfuls and Admirers to keep up the Faith. May God bless you!

The Circle of Life: https://oceansofblues.blogspot.com/

Ancestral Motivation • A podcast on Anchor: https://anchor.fm/gumaa-francis-lodongi

The Peak of Passion • A podcast on Anchor: https://anchor.fm/gumaa-lodongi

#Humanity! • A podcast on Anchor: https://anchor.fm/gumaa-lodongi5

Introduction

I am writing this book to address the deep-rooted issues within the epicenter of South Sudan and Sudan in regards to love, hatred, peace, and conflict: Poverty, Violence and Non-violence, Security, Discrimination, Human Rights, War and Justice, Fury, Freedom, Humanity, Communication, and Forgiveness. In addition to this, I talk about the historical biography of President Salva Kiir Mayardit, President Omar Al-Bashir, Dr. Riek Machar, Dr. John Garang de Mabior, President Jaafar Muhammad Nimeiry, and Dr. Hassan Al-Turabbi.

These subjects aren't only relevant and reflective of what the continuity is, that is globally traumatic and destructive to the original intent of Humanity. But can be prevented by any such measure that is of hope, faith, common understanding, mutual love, respect, and sense of belonging. As, for the common ground, we are firmly established in the human audacity, to face these differences and not battle or war one another but to feed the oneness that once was us and will always be irrespective of our creed, religion, faith, without the channeling of either evil or good that is in us.

I was born in Kosti, Sudan, in 1993 to a Latuko mother and father who disciplined me and taught me to love my neighbors and carry myself with the proper and protective manners. The reason I point out protection is that by loving

1

one another as a nation or as a binding whole, we create tremendous forces that shield us from unpredictable and unprecedented atrocities. My parents were and still are very religious and instilled in me the valuable principles of treating others as you would like to be treated, investing in the goodness of everyone, including everybody in the circle of life, sharing what you can to increase what's naturally not there.

I have entitled this book The Path to Peace: A never-ending struggle! The reason is that peace is never constant until heaven is finalized on earth but what we can do is manage by consistently repairing the torn tissues between us until it is fully fleshed out. It takes a lot of work, discipline, tenacity, perseverance, and broader perspective as we trust the process and allow it to enfold us as we journey through this treacherous and miraculous jungle that will at some time produce the fruits of our labors. The reason why we currently struggle for peace is that we suffer from greed, power, jealousy, envy, and endless lower consciousness traits that trap us in a world of illusion by which we cannot escape. Peace, on the other hand, is only possible by the release of our selfishness and service to our creator that is the majesty, one above all religions.

Think of it this way there is a land in which we live, and there are many trails leading to that infinite source (reservoir) where we lead individually with different methods of sustainability to obtain the same bucket of holy water. That should give us mutual respect and unconditional love through which we must be responsible for. Here's an interesting idea, we have to be responsible and vigilant of the crimes and vices happening in our country because it is destroying the fabric of our society. The government starts from the smallest of communities to the top of the hierarchy. That's why it is our duty as citizens to unite against all ineffective and toxic forces that attempt mercilessly to paint our faces to the tombs of false heroes and prideful warriors.

Additionally, I maintain we shouldn't be prideful. I understand that we don't have anything to offer to one another and compete on the global stage in a healthy manner. That is most certainly true, but at the same time, we must govern our unified country with humility. The way I like to call it, we are humble builders, not prideful builders. When you start building something, where do you begin from? The bottom. Good on you, do that, and we will live, and as we shall build the nation with humble heart, our success will never end. Let us believe. Let us refocus our energies. Let us reinforce ourselves. And let us be at peace victoriously. In Allah or Jesus Christ's name. Amen. Peace be unto you!

Anything is possible!

That's why I reiterate; it is our duty as citizens to unite against all ineffective and toxic forces that mercilessly attempt to paint our faces to the tombs of false heroes and prideful warriors.

Dedicated to father South Sudan and mother Sudan (united)

I love you so very much! My Faithfuls and Admirers.

- Gumaa Francis Lodongi

Chapter 1: Dr. John Garang

Colonel John Garang de Mabior was a Sudanese rebel leader who founded Sudan People's Liberation Army (SPLA), fighting a 22-year civil war against the northern-dominated Islamist Sudanese government. Dr. John Garang de Mabior became the Vice President of Sudan on the signing of the complete Peace treaty in 2005, immediately before his death. He was born into the Dinka tribe, educated in Tanzania, and graduated from Grinnell College in Iowa in 1969. He returned to Sudan and joined the Sudanese army, but left the following year for the South to join the Anya Nya, a rebel group fighting for Christian and animist rights in the South. The South was controlled by the Islamist north at that time.

A rebellion ensued by the decision created by the colonial British to join the two parts of Sudan at the time of independence was given to Sudan in 1956. That resulted in a full-fledged war in the early 1960s. In 1972, there was an Addis Ababa Agreement regarding the Sudanese President Jaafar Neimeiry, and Joseph, leader of the Anya Nya, signed the Addis Ababa Agreement that granted independence to the South. Rebel fighters, including John Garang, were absorbed into the Sudanese Army. Dr. John Garang was promoted to Colonel and was sent to Fort Benning, Georgia, in the U.S to be trained. He also received a doctorate in agricultural economics from Iowa State University in 1981. On his return to Sudan, he became deputy director of military research and an infantry battalion commander.

During the second Sudanese civil war by the early 1980s, the Sudanese government was becoming increasingly Islamic. These standards were in addition to the introduction of Sharia law throughout Sudan, an imposition of enslavement of black people by northern Arabs, and Arabic being the official language of instruction and education. When Dr. John Garang was sent South to pacify a new chaotic riot by Anya Nya, he instead exchanged sides and created the Sudan People's Liberation Movement (SPLM) and their military wing, the SPLA.

While Garang usually conveyed Marxist principles in politics, he was also a Christian by faith. In 2002, Garang started peace talks with Sudanese President Omar Al- Hasan Ahmad Al- Bashir, which culminated in the signing of the inclusive and complete peace agreement on January 9, 2005. As part of the agreement, Garang was made the Vice President of Sudan. The peace agreement was backed up by establishing a United Nations Mission in Sudan. U.S. President George W. Bush conveyed hope and faith that Garang would be a leader of great promise as the United States of America helped South Sudanese to be independent.

Several months subsequent to the peace agreement on July 30, 2005, a helicopter carrying Garang back from talks with the President of Uganda crashed in the mountains near the border. However, both the government of Omar Al-Bashir and Salva Kiir Mayardit, the new leader of the SPLM, scapegoated other people for the dulled visibility. That allowed doubts and mystery to surround the death of Dr. John Garang de Mabior. He is known to be a very powerful and influential politician, soldier, and overall a personality that can never be matched in terms of the incredible intelligence he exuded in his political endeavors and successful ventures. He will always be my hero, the hero of South Sudan and Sudan, and an exemplary global leader.

Chapter 2: President Jaafar Muhammad An- Neimeiry

President Jaafar Muhammad An-Neimeiry was born on April 26, 1928, and passed away on May 30, 2009. He was a Sudanese politician who served as the president of Sudan from 1969 to 1985. He was a military officer who rose to power after a military coup in 1969—developing a one-party state with his Sudanese Socialist Union as the only legal, political entity in the nation. Neimeiry pursued socialist, and Pan Arabist rules and closely collaborated with Gamal Abdel Nasser of Egypt and Muammar Gaddafi of Libya. In 1971, Neimeiry survived a pro-Soviet coup attempt, after which he became an ally to Mao Zedong of China, who gave him considerable military and economic support.

In September 1983, he applied Sharia law throughout his nation, revived outdated penal codes such as amputating the hands of thieves and fornicators, and the ceremonial emptying of liquor worth 5 million dollars into the Nile. Such trappings of righteousness failed to impress the Ansar or support his growing fortunes. He was forced to step down from office by a popular revolution in 1985.

Neimery's early career nearly resembled that of Libya's Muammar Gaddafi. In 1969 both young colonels rose from humble beginnings to become Sudanese state leaders overnight. They imitated and surpassed the secularist free officer's movement that got rid of the Egyptian monarchy in 1952. "Everything must change," declared Neimeiry when he ousted Prime Minister Ismail Al-Azhari out of office. His promise gained huge popularity with the citizens of Sudan after years of tribal tensions and segregation, coups, colonial neglect, and constitutional uncertainty. He was vigorous and idealistic and wrote a regional commentator Alex De Waal, persuading ordinary Sudanese to build their nation anew.

In December 1969, he committed Sudan to join a grandiose, pan-Arab federation with Libya, Egypt, and Syria. He later clashed with Gaddafi, saying: "He has a split personality- births evil." Instead, Neimery became friends with the Egyptian President Anwar Sadat and was the sole Arab leader to be by Sadat after Egypt's Camp David Accords with Israel in 1978. Sudan also got rid of its Soviet military advisers and became the second biggest African state to receive U.S. aid after Egypt. Neimeiry grew up as a loving footballer. He was the son of a postman born in the Wad Nubawi district of Omdurman near Khartoum. He received his education at Koranic and state schools and graduated from Khartoum military college in 1951. He was arrested constantly for subverting the government during the 1950s and 1960s.

After training in Cyprus, Libya, West Germany, and Egypt, he took a military course at Fort Leavenworth,

Kansas (1964-1966). As a ringleader of the 1969 coup, he abolished parliament, outlawed all political parties, and spearheaded a revolutionary command council. He then named himself commander-in-chief and defense minister and crushed an impending Ansar rebellion, slaughtering thousands near Aba Island on the Nile. Among the dead was Al- Hadi Al-Mahdi, grandson of the religious ruler who defeated Britain's general Charles Gordon at Khartoum in 1885.

Overall, President Jaafar Muhammad Neimery has politically appeared to the people of Sudan and the rest of the globe with his very stern and harsh revolutionary policies. However, I like to maintain He is a complexity of a great man who was put in the position of a challenge, beyond his efforts, of allowing independence to come to fruition and peace to prevail for all of our fellow citizens. Meanwhile, it was also a challenge for us to be willing enough to accept him for who he was, a political force that governed Sudan not out of an attempt to overrule as it may have seemed but as an opportunity to break barriers, enliven matter, and Humanity. As the saying always goes, judge the actions of the person and not the person himself. We should and must forgive President Jaafar Muhammad Neimery for what he has done because forgiveness is the only way towards the rehealing and restoration of our tissues, the binding of our wounds, and the resurrection of our souls.

Chapter 3: Dr. Hassan Al-Turabbi

Dr. Hassan Al- Turabbi is the main leader of the strict and literal Islamic movement of Sudan. Hassan Abdullah Al-Turabi was born in 1932 in the town of Wad Al-Turabbi. He led the Islamic fundamentalist, the National Islamic Front (NIF), which was the force behind bringing Sudan toward being an Islamic state based on Islamic law. Turabi, the son of an Islamic legal judge, went to the University of Khartoum, where he earned a law degree. He was then elected to resume his studies in Europe, where he took his first Master of Laws degree from the University of London before a doctorate in Laws from the distinguished University of Paris. He amassed a huge amount of solid academic qualifications, bringing them to the land of Sudan, where he became well renowned as one of the nation's leading experts on Sharia, or Islamic law.

Dr. Hassan Al Turabbi believed that the government and society of Sudan entirely wouldn't function Islamically enough unless it is rooted in the Sharia. Islam is a way of life, as he did put it, which he wanted to permeate every component of a state or a citizen's being. It would be unmanageable to have a Muslim state without the primacy of the Sharia. He always thought it was necessary and paramount to have sharia law in place as long as the non-Muslim minority in Sudan is highly sizable. The devoted

Muslims must always oppose the secular state, but Dr. Hassan Al- Turabbi made an exception. Because of his considerable foreign academic training and travel, he thought it was very much okay for him to have an influence on people and to make cooperation possible.

Turabbi's influence in the affairs of Sudan continued to grow till the time Colonel Gafaar Neimery took hold of power in the coup, which made him a force to be reckoned with. After the Neimery coup of 1969, Turabbi was the leading oppositional force, and he was jailed numerous times for his outspoken criticism of the regime. To Turabbi, the Neimery government was secular, unconcerned with Islamic issues; this, obviously, was Turabbi's main concern. In 1964 Turabbi claimed to be the Secretary General of the National Islamic Front, and his prestige as a noted legal scholar and as a spokesman for the Islamic State had spread throughout the Muslim world.

Neimery had to be careful in dealing with a man of Turabbi's stature, and in 1977 Neimery offered national peacemaking to his opponents. Turabbi accepted the offer and was released from jail. Next, he began a campaign to move the Sudan legal system toward one based on Sharia. He spearheaded an order that proposed numerous important transformations in the system, and in 1979 he accepted the position of the attorney general of Sudan, which he held until

1983. He quietened his Muslim opponents by being a pragmatist and pointing out that the fundamentalist NIF couldn't want a better position for one of their own.

By the end of Turabbi's tenure as attorney general, Sudan was moving toward Islamization of their legal system bringing it in line with the Sharia. The Neimery government chose a socialist and democratic way to lead; however, with the changes in the legal system, it was becoming certain that the move was toward Islamic and Koranic religious principles. During the previous months of the discredited Neimeiry regime, Turabbi was again imprisoned. This spared him criticism since he had served as attorney general (1979-1983) and advised on foreign policy (1983-1985). He was then released from prison after the fall of Neimeiry, which caused him to heighten his pressure on the new government to move Sudan toward a totally Islamic state.

In 1986, Turabbi led the NIF to a strong third-place finish in free elections. Between 1986 and 1988, Turabbi led the opposition to Prime Minister Sadiq Al-Madhi's government. However, in 1988, he entered the government as attorney general. He continued promoting Islamization in this capacity, but it also aggravated relations between the north and the discontented South. For two months in 1989, Turabbi served as foreign minister. He was ousted from the government for his unyielding opposition to not want to compromise with the South, especially with the Sudanese People Liberation Army (SPLA). In consequence, Turabbi left the government and traveled through the Islamic world, Europe, and the United States.

Due to having a notable stature as the spokesperson for how primary the sharia law was in the Muslim state, he was highly in demand as an engaging speaker. Dr. Hassan Al-Turabbi was a man of strategy, discipline, authority to execute sharia law so that the citizens of Sudan may follow a particular order of living standards that challenges traditional Islamic and Christian doctrines. This was certainly what no one would propose to do if they're in power. However, Dr. Hassan Al- Turabbi was very out of the ordinary in the sense that he was a fundamentalist trying to instill Islamic values and wisdom into youth and people of all ages as at that time, people lacked education due to civil war. In fact, most of the people were very reluctant to acquire education. The way he decided to follow through with his disciplinary measures to maintain peace and order didn't fail; rather, it could've certainly met our expectations or exceeded if he had properly applied his school of thought in the right manner. However, if you were to ask me how I feel about him, I would like to think he was a man of extraordinary genius with attribution to his extensive level of education. In that regard, his influence, whether it is considered good or evil, was all for the greater good of the

14

Humanity of Sudan, South Sudan, and the globe as a whole because his faith, devotion, and courage remained strong for our country.

Chapter 4: Poverty

Poverty is a fundamental reason for disturbing peace and conflict. There are several ways to measure peace and conflict in relevance to poverty. First, there is an understanding that you have to acknowledge, and that is when the economy of a community is failing, the tendency for everyone to seek out a resolution to either mitigate the economic issue or ultimately obliterate the issue entirely. That is done by realizing the means by which we are inherently connected and feel the sense of belonging that a rooted tree breathes the air that innately holds it together. When you are poor, you feel transported between different states of being, that is, the mind, the emotions, and the spirit that is the invisible and infinite source. I like to call it interconnectedness. Peace is felt and experienced this way because of the binding factor it assumes.

Peace is also the discovery of a simple life that is lived on little resources and more gratefulness. Poverty minimizes the overbearing amount of alliances and burdensome resources that take time to manage and care for. It also provides you with the tools to focus on the power of individuality or to turbocharge the community as a whole. As a result, peace is brought to one's present state, and therefore, you are able to comprehend eternity better. With respect to poverty, you gain endurance, patience, tolerance, and the ability to withstand suffering and pain. You build value when you are poor by knowing there is a sense of peace to develop in the comparison of patience and impatience when you're suffering. You also build value when you tolerate intolerance. There is peace that comes upon you like a dove landing atop a pillar. That is the acceptability of you being like the pillar who accepts being blessed. Just as the pillar stands firmly with forbearance awaiting the dove, you too should wait if you want peace to enter into your heart.

When you are poor, you are at rest from all the worldly troubles, and you are free from the chaos involving wealth. You are also peaceful when your rest is so complete that it engages your spirit like or as though the spiritual plane of existence is completely impacting the materialistic globe that is the earth. The state of poverty is rich because of your ability to comprehend the complexity of that greatness that involves you being so connected to the truthful Constance that is peace. Love results from poverty also because when you don't have as many resources or materials as others, there is more you want to have, and that is the camaraderie that you should have with fellow Humanity. The reason for this is because God says blessed are the meek for they shall inherit the kingdom of heaven. What that means is you will be blessed as a result of the underprivileged state that you are in because you always have love and kindness in your

17

heart that you want to share to create friendship, association, or alliance.

God said that we should always love one another as they have loved us. Because when we do this, we show God that we accept ourselves for who we are and what we are. In essence, we are the meek and selfless who not only shall inherit the earth but understand the purpose of life that is on earth. The purpose of life that is on earth is to accept ourselves as we accept others, and that is how peace flows into our hearts. When we live this way, we embrace our Humanity without any regard to social or economic status. There is a joy that comes with being poor. That pertains to the understanding you are underprivileged, and your time shall surely come. You wait for prosperity, just as the shore that is thirstily awaiting its huge wave.

One of the most negative consequences of poverty is conflict, and that occurs when there is a collision of power, greed, and jealousy. We are driven inside conflicts because we choose to strive for power above everything and neglect what is of value. That is the significance of being in collective power rather than individual power. Imagine being in a tug of war, and you are pulling the ropes away from the other group. You don't do it on your own but rather with a helping hand keeping in mind the objective is greater than you, so then you must rely on the power of sharing and collectivism to attain the objective that is inherently sought by everyone that is part of your team effort rather than just yourself.

Never be greedy, for God said there is so much for all of us at the table of plenty. Be altruistic so that you are able to receive in return if you do so in the first place. Imagine you and a group of people have a full plate of pie in front of you. How do you then decide who gets what or what gets what? Or even you might have to consider whether I or any of us involved have a choice in the matter. Well, then you must understand. Plenty, or abundance, requires all to make a contributive difference in obliterating greed and sharing their contributions to the cause.

Before I continue on with this subject, you should very well know that there is a huge difference between jealousy and envy. Jealousy is when you are resentful of the success somebody has in a relationship with someone else. And envy is resenting the success of others directly with no third party involved. However, let's talk about jealousy though in this case, being in a congregation of people or amongst few people or even dwelling on the affairs of others resurfaces bitterness, hatred, and ill will between you and that person. So the resolution is to see the value in what you don't have or possess, for that matter, as a reflection of what others have to keep the balance of acceptable humility. Do not covet what others have because you will forfeit what you have, so you ought to always hold on to your cherished possessions because they symbolize what true poverty is. That instills peace within you because poverty brings justice to issues entailing racism. When you are jealous, you feed the evil component of you because of the poor state you are in. You feel entitled to that success that others have with other people. Poverty puts you in a mental state where you feel entitled to everything else and everyone else.

In summary, when we observe these facts of peace and conflict in relation to poverty, we note a number of things. In one case, peace is measured not by how much you accumulate or amass but by achieving nothing in the nothingness that one should ultimately pursue. As for conflict, you find yourself in opposition to yourself and others and the environment because when you are poor, you disregard that fact in which you are actually feeling entitled to others and life as a whole. These two components of poverty create a sense of attachment, like two children still connected to their mother via the umbilical cord. Peace keeps you in tune with the things that matter most, that is, love and not luxury for all Humanity because we are really the same. Also, it isn't the money that makes the world go round and round but love and joy that comes as a result of being in appreciation and gratitude for the little you have so that you can know you are underprivileged and not poor and that there is actually a big difference between the two.

As for conflict, we are tethered to poverty because we are pugnacious, warlike, and desire to start to quarrel because of our false sense of entitlement. We develop a tendency for violence because we allow poverty to delude us into thinking what others have belonged to us and what others think of us matter to us. That causes us to live for others as opposed to living for our standards and appreciating the meager amounts of resources we have that shall be greater in due time. Another false notion derived from poverty is we should become an anarchist and attempt to overthrow our government because we feel our freedom is stolen from us. Well, you are completely wrong. Your freedom is unalienable. That means only God Himself, our Almighty Creator, is responsible for life, can end life completely and utterly; that is eternity. If a simple thing such as your right possession as a commodity has been taken from you or even your right, the most important thing is that you still have life. That implies you are still in control and are able to make a difference in your life by taking your commodity and rights back because your life is still intact, and our Almighty Creator never neglects us.

Chapter 5: Violence

Now when we talk about the phenomenon of violence, peace is a major key that resolves it and sheds light on it. There are a few components entailing the relationship between peace and violence. First of all we should ask ourselves, what is violence? How does violence come about? Who or what incites it? And why does it exist?

In my comprehension, as per Google dictionary, violence is behavior involving physical force or verbal force intended to hurt, damage, or kill someone or something. It comes about in many ways, one being that it can be caused by a misunderstanding or a disagreement based on an entitlement one, or the other person feels he or she has a share in the resources at hand. If a person feels this way, she or he is threatened in any kind of way, then they will react by self-defense or even be the ones to instigate trouble or problems that be considered violence. Because obviously, you are or would be hurting, or damaging or killing someone or something.

Violence exists because people aren't considerate or caring for each other in this life that we live in this wide globe. We are also not loving humanity or being adequately humanitarian that we can actually value compassion more over cruelty. We are too quick to take offense and too quick to offend others as opposed to letting matters slide and giving ourselves and the situations that we are present in take their course and be the transforming factor for how we develop close ties with each other. For instance, when you are in a huge queue to get into a grocery store and it is taking too long for your turn to come. Alternatively, somebody buds in and you want to fight or quarrel with that person because you feel entitled to the position that you are in.

In such circumstances, you become a failure to the golden rule and you forfeit the sensibility to understand the oneness that we originally are. If we choose to share the circle of life, our lives will turn out for the better. We will become successful because we take calculated risks rather than uneducated risks that can fail us and the economy in respect to our contributive society, of course.0

Peace is an assuring thing when we are facing violence head on in our lives. Peace is like living water that is the sustenance to our present state because it is either the barrier to violence or the complete destroyer of violence.

Let us talk about peace in regards to violence with it serving as a barrier unto it. Peace serves as a barrier to violence because it enables us to maintain our longevity or even at a very basic level, provides for us clarity to solve problems and discover new ideas. We can come up with visions for the near and very far-reaching future and can accomplish bountiful for our beloved nation.

Peace also serves as a barrier to violence because it gives us the ability to take notice of the hidden meanings of life that are very crucial to how we can improve relationships, the economy, our culture, and our tribal and religious differences. Peace can never be taken neither given unless we, the ultimate decision makers, allow others to take advantage of us or humiliate us. When we let others that are the outsiders abuse us and/or humiliate us, a disorder violates our moral character and reputation. That violation is the violence that only peace can rectify.

Violence, in my opinion, is what violates the rules and principles that bind us together. Violence is like a venom that can only be prevented by the psychology of love that we should shed for humanity rather than for our own selfish recovery. When you are in the face of violence, you should, by all means, not seek recovery for selfish reasons but instead for inclusive or altruistic reasons so that the payment of the violence that was applied against you can be repaid through the unconditional love that we must all share. Never seek revenge as a way to end violence and never start violence for the sake of violence.

First and foremost, you ought to never seek revenge as a way to bring an end to violence. Violence tends to be like a conversation or a tennis match that you would have with yourself against the wall. When you talk to someone, you will not only get a response, rather most likely even get a backlash. But when you talk with someone to resolve or reconcile you will certainly get them talking with you in return, and you two will have a very good and smooth conversation. In a tennis match against yourself, the ball is coming back to you according to how you hit the ball. If you hit it hard and fast, it returns to you the same way, but if you hit it gently and slow, the ball will come back to you at a tender pace.

Peace finds its way into the equation when you realize the greatest enemy that you have is you and the greatest battle you face is the context of the situation and not the answer to the situation. When you seek an answer to a situation, you are retaliating, but when you are contemplating the context of the situation, you are a history of everlasting peace. The greatest enemy you have is no one else but you, because whether you provoke or respond to a conflicting situation it is you yourself who bears the brunt or the force of violence. You have to understand as an individual that life is a reflection of what resides within you. Everything that you face in life is a reflection of what resides within you. And nothing else matters. Everything you face in life, whether it is violence or anything else, for that matter, your emotions, mind, and spirit which is the interconnectedness that brings peace, will not bring any peace unless you reconcile all issues within yourself.

Conflict and violence are similar. Conflict is the result of the violence that is either the damage a person is subject to or murdered. Meanwhile violence is the disorderly conduct or physical force that takes peace out of the equation. There are three types of violence in regards to conflict. The first one is verbal violence, the second one is emotional violence, and the third one is physical violence. Verbal violence is when two or more people are having contentious conversations that lead to one being hurt or both being hurt. For example, in a court case, when a defense attorney is arguing a case to defend their client, it ignites a fire and creates a storm between them and the prosecuting attorney who is defending their client, attempting to bring about a winning result for the client or justice and equality. Verbal, emotional, or physical violence erupts when there is a need for justice and equality.

There is also a need for a balance of mutual benefits regarding materials when people are being physically violent trying obtain the same salary or wage. For example, you are a woman working in a pharmacy or grocery store or a convenience store. Your main intention originally is to be paid just as equally as all the male employees you are working along with. Because it is constitutionally written that all women and men are to be treated equally in the eyes of our Almighty Creator and such should be the scale of justice. But men in positions of power abuse the scale of justice and equality for their own gain and hurt or damage or even murder women to unfairly obtain higher salaries.

Chapter 6: Nonviolence

In our previous chapter, we have covered violence and discussed it thoroughly. But in this chapter, we will talk about nonviolence. Nonviolence consists of some components that link it to peace.

One aspect of this link between nonviolence and peace is if you are in a situation where there is no violence or whatsoever. Peace might still not be there because peace and nonviolence aren't the same thing, even though they are actually similar. For instance, you live in a neighborhood where there is quietness, stillness and order. The duality of good and evil would still be there, affecting everybody else in the neighborhood, not noticeably of course but subtly or even energetically. Nonviolence and peace, in comparison, are not equal because nonviolence means even though there may be order and organization, humanity is not joyful, gratified, or even ecstatic about the current state of living. In such a case, the affairs amongst humanity may be tarnishing society in a way in which any irony is served but not the appearance.

Peace is when there is silent stillness, as though the water fountain is spouting water and nothing can be heard at all. There is an obvious appearance of the sight but only just motion of the water spouting, just like the neurons silently pumping blood within. Nonviolence is when in a society there is no damage, hurting, or killing towards humanity; physically, verbally, and emotionally. However yet, there is still no peace because there isn't gratitude applied or forgiveness practiced enough, which incites to delay progress.

You can ask why there is a requirement of forgiveness from humanity. It is because we have a past, present, and future. If there is no violence in the present moment, then that means we have forgiven ourselves. However, what we also need to do is forgive our previous history. We still don't practice gratitude, which is what would separate nonviolence from peace. If you don't thank the Almighty Creator for your god-given talents and skills, then you wouldn't have peace with your heavenly father. Hence if you live in a society where it is nonviolent there can be no peace at all within you and between our Almighty Creator.

There is another comparison between nonviolence and peace that I want to talk to you about. Peace and nonviolence can coexist of course, but also not coexist. The coexistence between nonviolence and peace is when we live in a community whereby we find it simple to adjust to the environment around us and what dwells within our hearts and minds. However, peace and nonviolence do not coexist because of the imbalance thereof. The imbalance is when humanity is full of regrets and taking life for granted to the degree that they fail to attain peace while there is nonviolence in the community or attaining the state of nonviolence while there is no peace.

Conflict is like gasoline on fire. It doesn't put it out but aggravates it. Nonviolence is like energy that transmits without any spikes. The connection or association I find with conflict in respect to nonviolence is that it doesn't blend with it, making it difficult for there to be peace. When there is no peace, it is hard to identify the current state that you're in and whether you actually have any issues to deal with at all. Therefore you are stuck in a time where there is no evolutionary cycle. I said nonviolence is like energy that transmits without any spikes. This is because when we are nonviolent or the environment we are in is also nonviolent, we can be unaware of it because of the presence of conflict in our lives.

Chapter 7: Discrimination

In the previous chapter we have discussed security, but in this chapter I will be talking to you about the subject of biases that is causing our nation to capsize. This discrimination crosses several planes such as racism, ageism, sexism, disability, profession, ethnicity, religious and caste prejudice. Racism has a very vital influence in our community, and society at large. Racism affects our social, political, cultural dynamics, etc. Dynamics when we choose to only love those who love us and hate those who hate us or against their innocence curse them. We fail in our aims to bring about a peaceful evolution for all Humanity when we fail to grasp the visceral concept of the oneness that binds our nation.

Racism is like the turbulence that you encounter far out into the seas it can either capsize the boat that you are riding on or raise it up higher slowly guiding you to the destination that you truly belong to that is the heavenly destiny. But before I fully discuss with you the details of racism and how it benefits us, let's first talk about how it is harmful to us like the honeybees in the forest stinking their surroundings but also giving away its beneficial honey to sustain the occupants.

Never judge others for if you shall judge people, others will judge you also. This means that racism flows like the river causing us to be the content of the flow. "Love your neighbor as I have loved you," our Almighty Father said, because when you do this you will see the true meaning of life, that your life is not only the same as another person's life but it is only but one life for we share the same time and space. Treat others as you would like to be treated. If you do this, you will see the worth for how you ought to care for yourself and maintain the precious living soul that is you.

I iterate this because when you treat another person shamefully, you damage the moral character of who you are and the balance that constitutes what you are. That is the eternally existential being who originally is deserving of mercy and grace. Be merciful, for your father is merciful. You should be merciful because it takes a thoughtful investment of you to show mercy unto others. This means that for what you so work hard for, that is the replenishment of your own soul, and your spirit also replenishes the emptiness of your fellow creation. Don't be too caught up in money for it is a trap like the web of a scorpion luring you into the scorpion's mouth.

Like I said earlier, money is the root of all evil, not the root of all peace because it forces us to lose sight of our priorities. That is our fellow Humanity who are in need of our care, consideration, kindness, mercy, compassion, and love. Be compassionate for other people so you can set an example of peace that knows joy and pride like the reflection of our heavenly skies unto itself. You should also be compassionate because it is a necessity to make our nature, reality, and existential matter heal and re-heal.

Compassion is the key not only to a Humanity's heart, mind, soul and spirit – the interconnectedness that brings peace – but it is also what engages our visual acuity to be able to not just perceive the goodness and holiness in others but to transform that which is unholy and atrocious. Love your enemies and do good to those who are different than you and who have cursed you and treated you with indignity. Your reward for that is not only in the Kingdom of Heaven but in the present moment too that is precious and desirable.

If we just solely love our enemies and do good to those who are different than us and who have cursed us and treated us with indignity, our reward will manifest in this reality. We shall understand the true nature of Humanity and our progressive pathways towards fair, just and equal future where no one will be neglected and everyone will be included in the circle of life.

In my opinion love is the greatest source of all that unites differences, blends similarities, and creates sameness of cultures, ethnicities, ages, genders, and overall caste. With love, you will be able to look and see, hear and understand, and have your senses entirely sharpened due to the blessings

33

you shall earn from the reciprocation of cares and consideration of your fellow Humanity. Love ensures us of the potential of what it is that we can do for our Almighty Creator that is communicating with him and hearing his words and obeying his commands. God said to us that we should obey his commandments that is first love and honor our mother and father, for life begins from our mother and ends with our father.

Ageism can be disheartening to the relationship we have with our fellow elders. I believe that in our society today, the youth is so much focused on matters that are not important and conducive to our ever-evolving development from the smallest of communities to the highest hierarchy of society. People of all ages excluding seniors especially children tend to not have respect and honor for their fellow elders because they don't want to understand the value that older generations have on life, the globe, and Humanity. They are careless about the cycle of birth, life, death, and rebirth and what impact evolution has on our present society at large.

This then derails the youth from associating or even connecting with their elders and inquiring them of the continuity of what life is. The youth also suffer as a result of their dishonor and disrespect towards elders because they forfeit their opportunities to become wise just as they are or even as they should be wiser than the elders so they can be the successor to the duties and responsibilities that structure our existential plane. Even young adults nowadays have gotten their priorities mixed up while not realizing they choose to engage in activities way inappropriate to their age because they just don't understand the values, wisdom, resources, and benefits that our elders can provide or bequeath. There is so much to be inherited from our elders that is the touch of Humanity that we take for granted. They possess the touch of love that once did bring us to this life and this universe. This touch can allow us to be reincarnated again even if we tap into it by sharing the companionship with our fellow elderly Humanity.

Elders can teach, educate, and explain to us the basic principles of how to accomplish our individual dreams and aspirations. That is why we should always seek the interests of our elders and the opinions of our elders. Our elders can be, as a matter of fact, like our sounding board, giving us advice at every turn. Better yet, they not only can be but they actually are our mothers and fathers physically, mentally, emotionally, and spiritually. So that is why it is significant for all of us to heed to their needs and wants first so that we can have the blessings of their incredible and powerful wisdom.

Sexism is like the codependent limb, one needs the assistance of the other to move normally and efficiently with great and thorough equality. Let us not be sexist because it is wrong in every respect to how we can function as one whole. Sexism is like the parallel universe. The first universe needs its parallel universe to cooperate and act accordingly so they can achieve the same purpose and aim that is to break barriers, enliven matter and Humanity. Just because we men once dominated the earth or continue to do so, it isn't our right to abuse this power because it can be taken away from us. This dominant power never belonged to us but to the infinite source and invisible source that is our Almighty Creator.

So my advice for you is, if you want to make the dynamics coherent and live in a functionable society, raise inclusivity for women just as you would take be inclusive of your passionate self and heart. Women don't dwell in our rational minds but in our ever-evolving and ever-flowing unconditional heart. We may be rational but we can also be emotional because our tears don't come from our brains but from our hearts when we lose our belongings, or even when we lose the possession of a car that once belonged to us. This is totally incomparable to the love that we can have for our women and the companionship we must nurture for and with our beloved women.

Women on the other hand have to see these sexist issues and try to work organically in resolving the tensions we are facing with each other. It takes two to tango. One limb has to take the initiative of walking or jogging to prepare the other limb for running a marathon. Women, you should never be afraid of the false consequences or the risks involved with confronting the discriminations men pit against you. You have to take initiative at home, work, school, and even in the battlefield that is your overall life for your wellbeing depends on it, as do your rights and privileges that express your womanhood. Humanity can and will make a mark on this universe so that you can be the true leaders not only because of your rational intelligences but also emotional intelligences that mainly has been neglected for far too long.

Disability is a major problem plaguing society because we able-bodied feel superior to those who are crippled. It is as if we are sitting on the highest chair and they are sitting on the plain ground. This is a very awful way to look at Humanity because it causes us to disengage from our precious and wonderful earth and what it attempts to reveal to us: that the crippled and the lame and the mentally ill are just like any of us. Their service to our global earth is unlike any other because it exemplifies that we should build with humility and live with humility for we are actually lowly rather than mightier than our Almighty Creator.

Peace is attained when you care for the sick and attend to the needy that is the blind. When you do this, you develop yourself as a good caretaker of our Humanity, guardian of our universe, and the guide to the infirm and the unseen.

With respect to ethnicity, there is so much tension boiling within the epicenter of South Sudan and Sudan. We are failing to grasp the unity that we should be because we are worried about our conflicting past and the traditions that we have lost and the time and space that is confounding our hearts. We need to understand our division was never based on war that we fought or the little quarrels we've had. It was based simply on time that it is the generational evolution that caused our division and also the resolution to our ever-rising tensions.

We need to take heed of time because time as is the past, the present and the future is the ultimate enemy. Suppose you fought with your brother, sister, or mother, or father over who obtains the inheritances of your grandparents. Then you all decide to hold grudges because of the overwhelming conclusion resulting in you not getting what you consider a fair share. In that case, you should know that it isn't the people that you are fighting or what you are fighting over that you are still angry and bitter at, it is actually the time, because when you look at it, before the conflict happens you are undivided with your family because the time was favorable to your unity.

Then when you look at it presently, as when this conflict happens, you have the time to blame because it was never favorable. Once the conflict ends, you decide to hold a grudge because of the entitlement that you feel towards the inheritance as like time hangs in the present moment without past and future. So let us not blame our brothers and sisters but most importantly our elders that is father South Sudan and mother Sudan, for if it wasn't for them, there wouldn't be life continuing for you younger generations. You need to understand that life depends on time and time depends on life and we are in control. If we fail to grasp time and appreciate it for the hardships and joys we have suffered and benefited from, then we can actually be slaves to time. This is the reason why we are behind the times. Our national existence never had to do with development at all but instead with time, because time is the deciding factor for everything. We must first take full control of that.

Religious discrimination is also a detriment to our society. We should understand that we should never discriminate against our fellow citizens or anyone else for that matter for their faith, religion or – even as awful as it sounds – their object of worship. Religion is a touchy subject, which means that it requires the touch of Humanity for us to appreciate the differences, similarities, sameness for that love created as a result of religion nurturing us. We shouldn't mock others for what they believe in and who they believe in. That is their God, which is ultimately our one majesty, the Almighty Creator, if we only can consider the love, kindness, compassion that our Humanity nature has engineered within us from the time of birth.

If we are born together and we die together, doesn't this mean that we share the same origin that is the infinite and invisible source? And if we truly do, why can't we share the same respect and honor and love for all religions that lead to that infinite reservoir where we can draw the holy water of sustenance that enables us to dig deeper into the complexities of life and resolve them?

As for the caste there are no untouchables, and there are no superiors, for we are all one and the same sharing the circle of life. Hate with hate only fuels the fire that should enlighten our perspective of the depth of Humanity and the depth of fairness and equality.

Chapter 8: Human Rights

Let us begin to talk about the violations of Humanity by considering that the Cambridge Dictionary defines the basic human rights generally as rights that all people should have, such as justice and the freedom to say what you think. Another definition that the Cambridge Dictionary asserts of human rights is the basic rights to fair and moral treatment that every person is believed to have.

Conflict ensues when human rights are violated due to the immoral and wicked inconsideration of people's voice, property, freedom, justice, equality, faith, individual and collective independence, existential entitlement, education, etc. We need to comprehend that in order to end these violations, we need to stand up for that most cherished, significant, and precious life that is what all of these violations are based on.

We need to understand that neither life nor rights or privileges can be taken away or given by human beings. It is only the eternity that is the creation that inherently knows no limitations. Therefore you should by all means know that when tensions such as political uprising occur, they affect the standards to what it is that is the potential of how we can ascend and accomplish the holy grail that is the peak of glory. For us, all this is important because knowledge-focused motives of peace are the most evidently true

41

evolution that we should desire for Humanity. Humanity doesn't understand itself either, that is why the cause of human rights isn't the rebels or the government that is at certain times innocent.

We forget that there are other parties involved. For example, basically speaking, say you are in a situation involving you and another person in a trades deal and you end up being ripped off in the deal. It leaves you penniless while the object of the deal that is yours was taken. And you end up blaming that person for this, unbeknownst to the parties involved in causing this trade between the two of you to go wrong. You would most likely hold a grudge with him or her, which is wrong because just as there is every problem in life, there is a solution.

What solves a problem is the root cause and not the surrounding causes. Just as when you are pulling the weeds surrounding a tree, you target the ones that are heavily rooted first, then you make your way to the rest of the weeds abusing the tree and its scent that is the soul created to live in harmony with complete freedom. That is the voice to hiss in the winds like all the national trumpets trumpeting our freedom so that we be founded in our original identities as South Sudanese and Sudanese.

We as national or global citizens face so much turmoil and hardships because we also just don't get it that these instances of turmoil and hardships starts with our own ignorance in not confronting these human rights issues facing us. Because we exaggerate the impacts of them so much, disregarding our Humanity power to restore order and peace if there ever was one or rectify our relationships with culprits of this violation. As for property, we are certainly entitled to what we have earned with our own hard and conscientious work. Just as there is false power in dictatorship and abuse of Humanity's rights, we humans also have power that is true and strong in the diligence. It is this power that we use to earn our properties such as homes, cars, places of work, and abstractly, success.

We also suffer from oppression that hampers our freedom to be educated as we like. This problem is a ruinage, not only to individuals but to the entire society including the government. Because education is the locomotive force that engineers our existence and moves all of us forward towards peace. As I stated previously, knowledge-focused motives of oneself with God and thy nation and additionally the universe are what develop that inner and outer peace that lasts forever and knows no boundaries because it engages our human hearts.

Chapter 9: War And Justice

During the history of rising tensions in Sudan involving invasion from Belgium, British, and other European countries and the Arabs, the Sudanese government found it very challenging to defend themselves against the setbacks imposed upon themselves by external influences. They caused Sudan to forfeit a sense of awareness about who they are as Humanity, government, and a nation. This lack of self-awareness is because the Sudanese government lacked a foundational structure due to the internecine warfare amongst the native tribes. The Belgians, British, Arabs, and several other countries took an interest in engaging in trades of gold, silver, diamonds, and all sorts of minerals and natural resources from Sudan. This eventually opened the doors for settlement in the native land.

As the trades carried on, commotions started between foreign settlers and the government of Sudan due to the rising racism, greed, power struggle, jealousy, envy, selfishness, and hatred looming over. These factors made trade relations difficult for everyone else and for all to love each other and try to see the purpose of unity regardless of race, gender, and national background. This ever-evolving tension of racism, sexism, ageism, and all kinds of discrimination led to the imbalance of power in the government, which furthermore erupted a civil war between the Arabs and the native Sudanese. The civil war was a result of Belgians, British, and other European countries retreating from our beloved nation Sudan due to the determined efforts of the native Sudanese military consisting of all ages. During this time of confusion, the French aggravated the civil war by seizing Bahr el Ghazal and the western Upper Nile up to Fashoda.

Furthermore, they annexed these areas to the French West Africa. It caused more conflict between France and the United Kingdom, which is known as the Fashoda Incident. Then France agreed to cede the area to the Anglo-Egyptian Sudan. Since 1898, both the United Kingdom and Egypt administered all of present-day Sudan as the Anglo-Egyptian Sudan. Still, Sudan's northern and southern regions were classified as divided provinces of the condominium. Later on in the 1920s, traveling between two zones that is northern Sudan and Southern Sudan required permits to ensure that it would be possible. Businesses from one zone into the other had to be feasible. In northern Sudan, Arab and English were the two major components of languages spoken in addition to the countless other tribal languages.

On the other hand, South Sudanese people mainly spoke English, Dinka, Bari, Nuer, Latuko, Shilluk, Azande, Acholli, and numerous other tribal languages of the native Sudanese. While this civil war persevered, the British discouraged Islam in the South where there was a constant arrivals of Christian missionaries coming to spread the message of our Lord Jesus Christ. Their main aim was to christianize the nation of Sudan completely. Because their aim was to spread the good news, they were allowed permission to stay and work to also help change the political circumstances.

The British prioritized developing the economy and infrastructure of the north mainly while the native Sudanese in part of southern Sudan was trying to structure their own government, heal the torn tissues between all of the tribes, and attempting to reclaim its victory by taking its country back again from all of the attempted colonizers and invaders. In February 1953, the United Kingdom and Egypt settled on a treaty providing Sudanese self-government and self-determination. The independence of the native Sudanese from the British came in 1954 with the inauguration of the first parliament.

On August 18 1955, the army in Torit, South Sudan revolted and war broke out. Although it was almost suppressed, it led to a low-level revolution by former Southern Rebels. It commenced the genesis of the First civil war in Sudan that is considered the longest civil war known to mankind, dating six decades or perhaps even longer if history serves correctly. On December 15 1955, the Premier of Sudan Ismail-Azhari declared that Sudan would alone announce its own independence unanimously. Afterward, the Egyptian and British governments viewed the independence of Sudan on January 1 1956.

The Arab-led Khartoum government reneged on a pact with Southern Sudanese people to create a federal system which would lead to a rebellion by Southern army officers that ignited seventeen years of civil war (1955-1972). In the earlier war era, numerous northern bureaucrats, teachers, and others such as officers were annihilated. Prime Minister Ismail al-Zhari of the National Unionist Party (NUP) controlled the first cabinet, who replaced the coalition of right wing political forces. In 1958, Chief of staff Major General Ibrahim Abboud removed the Parliamentary regime forcibly from power in a bloodless coup d'état following a time of economic challenges and political movements that hampered public administration. With respect to the civilian government, however, and well-known bitterness against army rule, a wave of uprising prompted in late October 1964 that forced the military to relinquish power.

This is the reason why Gen. Abboud didn't follow through with his promises to return Sudan to the civilian government. There was a coalition government of the Umma and National Unionist parties under Prime Minister Muhammed Ahmad Mahjoub that came in April 1965 due to the parliamentary elections of the temporary government that were followed by the Abboud regime. Between 1955 and 1969, Sudan had a sequence of governments that demonstrated beyond doubt that they could either agree on a permanent body of law or deal with issues of factionalism, economic delay, and ethnic discordance. However, after the early post-independence, governments were overpowered by Arab Muslims who viewed Sudan as an Islamic Arab nation.

In fact, the Umma and the NUP suggested in the constitution of 1968 that Sudan was arguably first an Islamic oriented constitution. The struggle continued when the coup leader, Col. Jaafar Nimeiry became prime minister, and the new regime destroyed parliament and banned all political parties. This discontent developed to the degree of a second coup d'etat on May 25, 1969. Huge disagreement between Marxist and non-Marxist parties working within the ruling military coalition resulted in a shortly successful coup in July 1971, which the Sudanese Communist Party led. Then the anti-communist military elements brought Col. Jaafar Neimeiry to power all over again.

In 1972, the Addis Ababa treaty incited a discontinuance of the civil war between the north and the South to the scale of self-government. This led to a ten years break in the civil war. Until the early 1970s, Sudan's agricultural yields were mainly dedicated to interior consumption. Furthermore in 1972, the Sudanese government became more western inclined and created blueprints to export food and cash crops. But, the prices of goods reduced throughout the 1970s, making economic issues for Sudan difficult. The money that was spent on mechanizing agriculture caused so much debt of all the costs associated with buying and selling food and cash crops.

During this time, the International Monetary Fund (IMF) negotiated a structural adjustment program with the government. This furthermore endorsed the mechanized export agriculture sector. Which caused more great economic problems for the pastoralists of Sudan. In 1976, the Ansars attempted to strike a bloody coup d'état. And then President Nimeiry met with Ansar leader Sadiq al Madhi, in July 1977, opening the way for reconciliation. More than hundreds of political prisoners were released, and in August, President Jaafar Nimeiry reprieved all of his dissident opponents. In 1983, the second civil war in the South ignited again after the government's policy that Islamified and brought Islamic law into an institution. Other things also happened, such as following several years of battling with the government ending up accommodating southern groups.

A period of drought came in 1984 and 1985, where more than a million people were discouraged and threatened by famine, especially in the western part of Sudan. The government, as a consequence, attempted to hide the circumstance internationally. There was a triggering of the first demonstrations of negotiation by the regime with the IMF, based on its request to increase the prices of basic necessities as announced in March 1985. On April 2, eight unions called to mobilize and politically strike up until the current regime would be abolished. Then the third huge protest hit Khartoum, the country's economic and trade centre; this strike immobilized institutions and the economy of Sudan and South Sudan.

On April 6, 1985, a cohort of military officers led by Lieutenant General Abd ar Rahman Siwar adh Dhahab overthrew Nimeiry, who sought asylum in Egypt. Three days later, Dhahab authorized a fifteen-man Transitional Military Council (TMC) to rule Sudan. Sadiq Al Mahdi formed a united government in June 1986 with the Umma Party, the Democratic Unionist Party (DUP), the National Islamic Front (NIF) and four southern parties. Unfortunately, Sadiq showed to be a lame leader and unable to govern Sudan. The Sadiq regime was typified of factionalism, corruption, personal rivalries, scandals, and political unreliability. With less than a year in office, Sadiq Al Mahdi discharged the government because it had suffered failure to draft a new code of penalization to replace the sharia law. He reached an understanding and agreement with IMF to end the civil war in the South or devise a plan to draw inward compensations from Sudanese expatriates. Sadiq then, however, formed another coalition government that proved to be ineffectual to attempt to retain the back-up of the DUP and the southern political parties.

Moreover, the government and southern rebels started to negotiate a conclusion to the war. However, a coup d'état caused a military overthrow, which brought the military into political power that was not overall interested in compromise. The leader of the junta, Omar Al-Bashir strengthened his resolve and power over the next few years, declared as the President of Sudan and South Sudan. The civil war displaced more than four million southerners. Some fled into southern cities, such as Juba; others ran as far north as Khartoum all the way into surrounding countries in the northern region such as Ethiopia, Somalia, Uganda, Kenya, etc. The people that fled the war in Sudan and southern Sudan did so due to the shortage of food, or the inability to earn money to feed themselves. Malnutrition and starvation had become widespread.

No one was investing in the South, which resulted in a country devoid of hope and faith. Other parties, such as the international humanitarian organizations, would call it a lost generation who lack educational opportunities, entry to basic health care services, and little potential for productive work in the not so big and weakened economies of the South just as well as the north. A new rebellion of Sudan Liberation Movement/Army (SLMA) and Justice and Equality Movement (JEM) groups in the western region of Darfur commenced. The rebels accused the central government of failing to care for the Darfur region, although there is unreliability in respect to the rebels' goals, and whether they just seek a better position for Darfur within Sudan, or outright withdrawal.

As much as both the government and the rebels have been accused of calamities in this first and second civil war, however, the Arab militias (janjaweed) have absorbed most of the blame. The rebels believed they were allied with the national government. They allege that these militias have been engaging in ethnic cleansing in Darfur, and the fighting put more than hundreds of thousands of people into exile, many of which have sought asylum in neighboring Chad and some even suffered deaths at the hands of the rebels, militias, and both southern Sudan and Sudanese government. There are varied numbers of casualties, ranging from under twenty thousand to several hundred thousand dead from either direct physical combat, suicide, or starvation and disease inflicted by the conflict.

Lastly, as justice is concerned, we have to consider where we stand amid the civil wars that we have faced as a nation. They previously clashed with each other and within surrounding countries of the globe that attempted to seize the nation of Sudan from its original citizens and inhabitants. Because when we allow ourselves to think of the history of what we traumatically went through, understanding it sensibly, we can break from the vicious cycle of birth, death, and rebirth based on ruthless hatred that we harbored towards each other. The only way we can break from this vicious cycle is by being honest about who struck the first blow and who retaliated, and on what grounds these strikes were based. Then by these means of analysis, justice will be served for every person involved, dead or alive. This is the only way for us to find peace and maintain it. We must all share understanding and agreement to figure out what works best for our villages, municipalities, counties, states, national and global society at large.

When we look at the bigger picture, we realize that since the war was never self-inflicted or instigated by one person, there becomes a measure for how civilized we should and must be to become one coherent Humanity. For instance, if we continue to be pugnacious towards each other or put one another at harm, this can spiral and lead to an ever-long and repeated history of bloodshed and war by which it would be hard for a person to become self-aware all over again and regain a sense of individual, national or global pride. Therefore war cannot continue, and it shouldn't ever because the globe thrives on Humanity just as the soil thrives on photosynthesis.

As Sudanese people, we should reconcile with each other and forgive each other, but also other countries who faulted us. That way, the same manner this war was initiated can come to an end with the same intensity of efforts involving mercy, love, and compassion. Because with love as the greatest source of inspiration, we can redeem ourselves from our current dire conditions to a higher awakened state. A state where we not only know ourselves, restore our pride, but also reunite to rebuild the nation of Sudan and make amends with our fellow neighbors.

Chapter 10: Freedom

In the 1990s, Dr. Hasan Al-Turabi Islamified Sudan under the national Islamic front. He transformed education and based its focus on the glory and praise of Arabs and Islamic culture. This included forcing children to memorize the Quran at school along with adults at temples as well as at home. During this decade, a law was enacted that ensured the replacement of school uniforms with combat gear; students were to be engaged in paramilitary drills. Police officers that were religious in the capital made sure that women were covered with a veil, particularly in government offices and universities. The once relaxed and normal culture became much harsher, with human rights groups alleging a production of torture chambers known as ghost houses used by security agencies. A war against non-Muslims and Christians was declared a jihad.

In the Sudanese revolution of December in 2018, massive demonstrations started after the government of Sudan decided to multiply three times the price of goods at a time when the country was dealing poorly with a severe shortage of foreign currency. Additionally, a convergence of opposition groups made a united coalition to oust President Al-Bashir, who had been in power for more than 30 years and refused to step down from office. More than 900 opposition persons and protesters were arrested because of the government retaliation. According to the Human Rights Watch, the death toll approximately reached 40 people even though the number was greater than that according to local news and reports of ordinary people.

On April 11 2019, the demonstrations resumed after his government was overthrown following a massive meeting in front of the Sudanese Armed Forces' main headquarters. Then they ordered the arrest of President Al-Bashir and declared a three-month state of urgency. Over 100 people died on June 3 after security forces scattered the assembly using tear gas and live ammunition in what is known as the Khartoum Massacre. The massacre resulted in Sudan's suspension from the African Union. Sudan's youth had been reported to be controlling and directing the protests. The protests came to an end when the forces for freedom and change (an alliance organizing the protests) and Transitional Military Council (the political Agreement and the August 2019 Draft Constitutional Declaration).

The government spurred all these events of disorder, chaos and dictatorship that loomed over the Sudanese and South Sudanese citizens. These events brought about the lack of freedom that devastated the entire population of Sudan and the South. Hope and faith were bleak, given how diminished the free will and autonomy of individual there was. Sharia law forcibly attempted to snatch our rights and privileges. However, because we have had a lack of liberty regardless of how much we have been dictated, and have been compressed against our will, we still to this day have our certain unalienable rights such as justice, liberty, and prosperity.

When there is a lack, there surely can be abundance. We weren't exactly characteristic of a lack of freedom as we were never deprived of it. We were though deprived of the ability to self-defend. It has become our way to be abundantly rest assured on the optimistic future of the independence and peace that we seek. We have hopes it will surely come our away, just as the ocean waves carve a channel into the land of milk and honey and the land of cush.

Chapter 11: Humanity

What is Humanity? What does it comprise of? A constellation of people who are selfless and caring towards others of different race or people of their own race in order to surmount racism, sexism, ageism, and all kinds of discrimination.

Since the beginning of time, humans have clashed and fought in the battlefields due to greed, jealousy, envy, selfishness, and struggle for wealth and power. This continued to repeat itself throughout evolution, causing there to be missing pieces of the potential of what could've developed: our measure to selflessly reach out to others and express love for them irrespective of what or who we worship, what our skin tone or color looks like, and what we prioritize as our individual and common objectives.

To be human is to err, but to be a Humanity is to be christlike. With that in mind, we must rid ourselves of the toxicity that is our human nature, for it causes us to sin; however, we should be a Humanity for it unveils the divine aspects of ourselves to become christlike. For if we are christlike, we can conquer racism and evolve throughout time to bring about heaven on earth. Just as there are many principles to sinning, there is the overall solution of reconciling with love. That is the greatest source of inspiration, love. That is god dwelling within us since the time of birth. Loving each other is of paramount standard to sharing the circle of life so that the globe may be devoid of war and conflicts. The circle of life is like one big pie that serves every hungry and eager individual willing to share in the feast without monopolizing or taking more than their fair share.

Being Humanity is accepting your present scenario regardless of whether it is problematic or not. To allow yourself always to see the positive and brighter aspects of matters, even though what you are facing is very detrimental. Having this perspective as a nation, we can become exemplary to lead the way for the rest of the globe to witness how we overcame hurdles greater than ourselves, placing ourselves in the pantheon of greatness. While on the other hand, if we remain as inhumanity as we have always been, we may not be able to see over the issues that plague us. We then scapegoat others for falling short of our own victories.

Chapter 12: President Omar Al-Bashir

President Omar Al- Bashir was born in January 7, 1944 Hosh Wad Banaqa, Sudan. He was a Sudanese military officer who led a revolution that got rid of the elected government of Sudan in 1989. He served as President of Sudan from 1993 until 2019, when he was ousted in a military coup.

Al-Bashir was born and raised into a peasant family that eventually moved to Khartoum, where he became the recipient of secondary education. Consequently, he joined the army. He went to a military college in Cairo, Egypt and fought in 1973 with the army of Egypt against Israel. He then came back to Sudan where he attained quick promotion. In the mid 1980s, he became the leader in the Sudanese army's crusade against the rebels of southern Sudan. The President didn't like how the country was operating and led a victorious coup in 1989. He became the head of the revolutionary command council for national salvation which ruled the country.

Dr. Hasan Al-Turabi supported him, a muslim extremist and leader of the National Islamic Front (NIF). Together, they started to make the nation of Sudan Islamic, and in March 1991, introduced the sharia law. This decision furthermore highlighted the division and segregation between the North and the animist and Christian South.

In October 1993, the revolutionary committee divided, and Bashir was selected as President of Sudan. He stayed in military rule and was affirmed as President by an election held in 1996. Bashir's ally Turabi was elected by mutual agreement as President of the National Assembly. On June 30, 1998, Bashir signed a new body of law that removed the suspension of political parties. In December of that year, however, he used military tactics to get rid of Turabi, who he assumed was conspiring against him.

On March 12, 2000, Bashir announced that there would be a three-month state of emergency, which, by stages, he thereafter extended indefinitely. After the December 2000 elections in which he was once again confirmed as President, he absolved the cabinet. President Omar Al-Bashir faced a degree of popular unrest that commenced in December 2018 and continued into the following year unprecedented. It started as a small coincidental demonstration over outrage with the country's struggling economy and how its affecting Sudanese living standards eventually turned into a larger-scale organized anti-government marches and demonstrations. As a result, many demonstrators and opposition leaders asked for Bashir to step down. He refused, stating he would step down only by referendum.

In February 2019, in the face of continued protests, Bashir took several actions, including declaring an emergency, absolving the federal and state government, appointing a new prime minister, and prohibiting unauthorized demonstrations. This did little to stop the orderly demonstrations. In March, he left his position as head of the NCP and promised to hold a dialogue with the opposition and enact reforms. Bashir would still not give up the office though the protests continued.

The largest protest of the movement up until now took place on April 6, 2019, as demonstrators marched to the military headquarters in Khartoum, the capital, and remained there for days. Security forces made harsh attempts to break up riots, which were met with violent resistance from sections of the military that moved to protect the demonstrators. Their actions depicted that Bashir could no longer think that he had the unwavering support of the country's varied security and military forces.

On April 11 2019, a military coup saw Bashir overthrown and placed under arrest. He was then removed to the Kober prison in Khartoum. Within that same month, they found so much money in his home that it led to formal charges against him for having caused acts of major corruption. He was convicted in December 2019 and sentenced to two years in a reform facility rather than a prison. Sudanese law did not allow individuals older than 70 years to serve time in prison. In the meantime, in May he was charged with the causing and involvement in the massacre of protesters earlier in the year during the demonstrations against his rule. Bashir also faced charges for his role in the 1989 coup that brought him to power that trial started in July 2020.

We are aware of the President's history of bittersweet relationships with his cabinet, legislative assembly, the military, and the civilians. Despite that, he was, in my opinion, also a great man because he remained courageous enough to be tenacious and determined to remain in the office regardless of the opposition. He respectfully stood for his own political ideologies, which he wholeheartedly believed would bring change, either for bad or for good. And in this case, as I like to judge the whole political spectrum of when he was in office, he most certainly remained steadfast to the people of Sudan when we needed him the most. Loyalty is never perfect. It is imperfect because of the challenges we face as one ever-evolving Humanity.

Chapter 13: President Salva Kiir Mayardit

President Salva Kiir Mayardit was born in September 13 1951 Akon, Gogrial district, warrap state, Sudan, which is now South Sudan. He is a southern Sudanese rebel leader fighting for the (SPLM) who in 2011 became the first President of the newly independent country of South Sudan. He has been serving for the partially independent region of southern Sudan while at the same time holding the position of first vice president in the national government of Sudan (2005-11). He has held the chair of the Sudan People's Liberation Movement (SPLM) since 2005.

Kiir grew up as a Christian and was born into a Dinka family in the southern region of Sudan. From 1955 to 1972, he joined the ANya Nya, a southern separatist movement, in the fight against the northern-based Sudanese government. After the fighting stopped, he was enlisted into Sudan's national army and eventually attained the rank of lieutenant colonel. When the tensions resumed in 1983, Kiir and others, such as Dr. John Garang de Mabior along with other soldiers, deserted the Sudanese army in favor of the (SPLM/A) which became the most important southern rebel group fighting against the northern-based government.

Within the (SPLM/A), Kiir was one of the top deputies of Garang's. He eventually held the position of commander and deputy to the SPLA council. He also held the portfolio for domestic and foreign affairs/intelligence. When divisions within the (SPLM) and (SPLA) surfaced in the 1990s and early 2000s, Kiir was an important mediator who managed negotiations between disagreeing factions. He also vitally participated in negotiations with the northern government, ultimately leading to the 2005 Comprehensive Peace Agreement (CPA) that ended Sudan's second civil war. Because of the terms of the (CPA), the semi-autonomous region of southern Sudan was developed in 2005.

On July 9, 2005, Garang was named President of the region as well as first vice president in the Sudanese national government. After his unexpected death later that month, Kiir took over both of his positions. Before the 2010 national and regional elections, speculations erupted about whether Kiir would choose to run for President of the country or President of the region. He chose the latter and almost received 93 percent of the vote to continue serving as southern Sudan's President. Kiir also continued on his ability to be the first vice president of the national government.

Another condition of the (CPA) was that a referendum should be held on whether southern Sudan should remain part of Sudan or become an independent country. The southern Sudanese people voted in January 2011, with the results overwhelmingly for autonomy. When the South faced secession on July 9, 2011, Kirr became the first president of an independent South Sudan.

Kiir faced many hurdles, including the overbearing assignment of creating a much-needed infrastructure to support the incipient state coping with lack of food security. He also managed the influx of refugees returning after several decades of civil war. He also dealt with continuing fights between the (SPLM/A) and other southern rebel groups, escalating tribal violence and going through South Sudan's risky relations with the government. This was especially with regard to contested regions along with their mutual border, which proved to be contentious in the years following autonomy.

Kiir also faced growing conflicts within the (SPLM/A), which evidently throughout 2013 culminated in an incident on December 15 that Kiir claimed was a coup attempt by his former vice president and (SPLM/A) rival, Dr. Riek Machar. Machar denied the accusation but soon took the lead of rebels combating Kiir and the (SPLM/A)-led government. The fighting rapidly divided everybody else when tensions inflamed between Kiir's ethnic group, the Dinka, and Machar's ethnic group, the Nuer. These tensions spiraled into a civil war that, despite global conciliation efforts in 2014 and 2015, revealed a small sign of ending in spite of the peace treaty signed by both Kiir and Machar in August 2015. Presidential and legislative elections were due in 2015, however, because of the ongoing violence, Kiir's term as President was lengthened by three years as the terms of the legislators confirmed.

Some improvement in ending the civil conflict seemed to have been made in April 2016. This was when the transitional government finally initiated the August 2015 peace agreement after much delay. This then brought back Dr. Riek Machar to the government to hold the position of first vice president.

To conclude this chapter, President Salva Kiir Mayardit's main focus was to carry on the legacy of Dr. John Garang de Mabior with respect to maintaining the independence of South Sudan and governing it as a just and prosperous nation with an opportunity for the citizens of Sudan to enjoy their unalienable rights such as justice, liberty, and prosperity. However, he also wanted to create his own legacy by evolving independence and bringing peace to the nation of South Sudan and mending ties with our fellow neighbors, including Sudan. This, to me, is a very honorable responsibility that we as citizens of South Sudan and Sudan and the Sudanese diaspora specifically have chosen to disregard and take for granted.

I think a lot of what goes in the office of a President has to do with not just the President and his cabinet but how the collective citizens of the state see him. What he has been depicted as has all been due to the projected vision of the expectations we set for the President of the most potentially abundant nation on earth. This false expectation tainted his image. However, as I'd like to maintain, he has always meant well. He has proposed to do his very best in regrouping the nation, maintaining independence, bringing peace, and reopening doors for all of the Humanity of South Sudan to re-enter as they wish to return.

Chapter 14: Dr. Riek Machar

Dr. Riek Machar was born in 1951 in his hometown of Leer in the oil-rich Unity State from the northern part of the country. His father was a chief of his clan, and he is a Presbyterian. Dr. Machar achieved his bachelor's degree in 1977 in Engineering from Khartoum University. He then got accepted into the United Kingdom with a scholarship. He then also earned his Master's degree in Production Management and Manufacturing Technology from the University of Strathclyde in Scotland. He further went on to obtain his Ph.D. in Strategic Planning In Industry from the University of Bradford in the United Kingdom.

Dr. Machar was a politician and an activist from the days of his secondary school in Sudan in late 1960s; an activism he also resumed during his education studies in Sudan and in the United Kingdom by 1983 before obtaining his Ph.D. in 1984. He joined a newly created (SPLM/SPLA) in 1983 under the leadership of late chairman Dr. John Garang de Mabior. Machar engaged in developing the first office for the movement in Addis Ababa, Ethiopia, and later on its humanitarian wing in Kenya and further on. After spending time in military training in Ethiopia and being commissioned as Major in SPLA, he became the Zonal Commander for Western Upper Nile and Southern Kordofan from mid-1980s. He was promoted to the rank of General in SPLA. He also became a member of the former political/Military High Command in the movement.

Machar was a democratic federalist who was among the leading members of (SPLM/A) and advocated for the rights of people of South Sudan to be self-determined. The advocacy became his main goal for decades all the way through his political struggle as a leader. This was after the Comprehensive Peace Agreement (CPA) was signed in 2005 between the (SPLM/A) – led by late Dr. Garang – and the Sudanese government – led by former President, Omer Hassan Al-Bashir – and after the inappropriate death of Dr. Garang three weeks after taking a solemn oath of office as President of the semi-autonomous government of South Sudan. Dr. Riek Machar took office as the vice president and then deputized under the current President of the Republic of South Sudan, his Excellency Salva Kiir Mayardit. He was the former vice president, then promoted to replace Dr. Garang as President of the government of South Sudan.

Kiir had competed for presidency in 2010, during the period in which Garang won the regional government's presidential election with a large-scale triumph. Machar as vice president was also put in charge of the high-level executive team to implement the Comprehensive Peace Agreement with Khartoum, co-chairing the joint team with vice president Ali Osman Taha.

He later on also chaired the southern Sudan high-level referendum task force, which prepared the people for the conduct of the referendum vote to make a choice between the unity of the Sudan and secession of South Sudan. Consequently, the right to self-determination was completely and successfully exercised in an internationally monitored referendum on January 9, 2011, in agreement with the CPA. The people of South Sudan overwhelmingly voted for independence from Sudan, with over 98% of the votes in favor of South Sudan being independent. This led to the declaration of the nation's independence on July 9, 2011, by H.E. President Salva Kiir.

When South Sudan obtained independence, Dr. Machar was reconfirmed as the vice president of the newly born Republic and currently the first vice president in agreement with the Revitalized Agreement on resolving the tension in the Republic of South Sudan.

Chapter 15: Communication

Communication is a vital component for the operation of a government of South Sudan and Sudan to be democratic. Since we have been engaged in two civil wars, we have retrenched from our potential to be a coherent whole. We can continue to hearken to our previous hurts and regrets of how we antagonized ourselves and demonized others. But then we leave no room to reconcile with ourselves first and foremost and our fellow neighbors. Your neighbour may be the person in the parliamentary office next to you or the person you're working in the oil field with. Or even that very person with whom you want to collaborate with in order to make all things possible for South Sudan, Sudan, and the rest of the globe to flourish and prosper. This is why I state that we must communicate, especially in the government.

The root of all evil is money, which is what makes the world go round and round. However, communication is the solution-based to put out all forces of evil, whether that may be money or deriving from money, causing us to clash. There is a power struggle and there is a struggle for wealth, but there is also the need to love one another as Allah has loved us, and the sense of belonging with which we need to cooperate and synchronize.

Personally speaking, I've learned in life that communication goes a long way, not only in dire situations, but in circumstances where you need to be open and willing to listen and speak. That is how you may exchange evolutionary and inspiring concepts with your fellow Humanity. For instance, imagine you're in a parliamentary session and you're sitting down at your own desk, afraid to speak up and share your concerns on either national or global affairs. How then can you debate with your fellow congressional or parliamentary members if you were asked to come and speak. What I am trying to say is, our voice has immense power. It can either bring upon death or life. If you used the responsibility of your voice with incredible authority, you can most certainly succeed in voicing your concerns and changing the community, society, nation, globe, and the entire universe with just a voice that once used to quiver at the sound of threats aimed against you.

Now you would be able to rise up and allow others to follow in your leadership and also rise with the pitch and tone of your voice bold that you feel courageous enough to use by trusting and deepening your faith in our Lord Jesus Christ. I know that with every opportunity to community, there needs to be a leader to initiate that communication. But what you need to consider first of all is anyone can be a leader as long as they are willing to be listeners and followers first.

You are to ask me who would then speak if everybody are listeners and followers. Well, there is the holy spirit of silence that speaks to us and prompts us to notice issues surrounding us and infecting us. If we really do listen to that holy spirit of silence, we can become great speakers communicating what our deepest core of being underlie, that is our dreams and hopes for a better and promising tomorrow.

Imagine a civil war such as the one we experienced that lasted six decades. It can be the contributing factor in making us feel hopeless, depressed, and very aggressive. However, we can restore ourselves from it all completely by being optimistic. Communication or just speaking up for the sake of speaking makes a whole lot of difference in our lives. It has a therapeutic nature to dissolve all the underlying tensions facing our economic, governmental, business, social, political, infrastructural, scientific, legal, etc. concerns. Communication builds familiarity and creates a sense of a balance that we can't deny. The fact that we can't deny it reasonably defines how paramount and life-evolving relationships are.

Relationships are all based on trust, and trust is most seldom created by the ability to speak and communicate your point of view to the person next to you. When you do so, you go without neglecting that person or even his agenda in ensuring you transfer the power of voice. If communication breaks, there is always the redemptive ability for us to reawaken ourselves and reset the motion by refocusing on what matters most and rechannelling our efforts to make everybody we come into contact with great.

The power of communication is the power of politics which I will be publishing in a book sometime in the near future. The power of communication allows the feasibility for the power of politics to take place. For what is the ever-empowering democracy that is influential to everyone as long as the citizens of South Sudan and Sudan entirely participate in voting to elect whomever they are favorably inclined towards?

Chapter 16: Forgiveness

In times of calamity that we've faced, there is one and only way for us to see the glory of God, and that is by forgiving each other and ourselves for purported or unintentional damages we have suffered. Forgive so that you may be forgiven. When you forgive, doors of opportunities open to show the potential that love of God has in heaven for us, which can be showered upon us. When you forgive a little, you will love a little, and when you're forgiven so much, you will love so much.

The measure with which we have sinned against each other as South Sudanese and Sudanese, and our fellow neighborly countries attempting to colonize us, it raises the standards for how much we are capable of growing. We are latently able to be the beacon of hope and inspiration for the younger generations to witness and become empowered as a result of our past. Civil wars or even colonial clashes are the rough stone against which a sword is chafed and sharpened. Let's realize how much we have become sharpened due to the civil wars or even colonial clashes. We willingly care about the fact it has sharpened instead of how much it has burdened us.

Forgiveness doesn't start with what or who we should improve our relationships with. It is rather the why to how we can better our relationships. When we understand it is the why, then we are that much sincere to reconsider forgiving others and ourselves for our previous wrongdoings. By forgiving, we liberate each other and give each other the power to redeem from the vicious cycle of karma that is birth, death, and rebirth. When we don't forgive each other or ourselves, we put too much pressure and pit judgment against one another and ourselves. This is why the root of evil seeps deeper into the soil, causing more roots to reproduce other bad fruits or even come to a self-obliteration. This can be detrimental, especially in our own current political, cultural, economic, and infrastructural tensions that delay our progress in forward engineering.

Conclusion

Summarily, no matter what we grapple or deal with, from the smallest of a quarrel to a physical fight between two or more individuals or even an aggressive civil war, it can as a whole be detrimental to the preservation of our history, present liberty, and prosperity of the future. That's why we need to refocus and harness again our energies into the things that matter to us, that is, the decision to always give up our arms and let go of our impetus to retaliate. We should instead seek a means to achieve our common objective, that is renegotiating our terms with our fellow neighbors who may have had wanted to seize our nation or not. If yes, we could put a stop to the corruption of international trades we were having with them. The revised terms with which we carry international trades with them could help all of us instead of one nation or only just a few. Had we been able to do this in the past, our past colonized nation wouldn't have suffered from the consequences of colonization.

However, since we all live on one planet earth, there is freedom whereby we can trade with other countries. As long as we are civil and respectful of each other's personal boundaries, we can always get along with each other and live in harmony. Allah and Jesus Christ have always given us this lesson. Peace isn't attained when someone invades resources or the residence of an individual. It comes when we appreciate what we have as individuals or nations to the extent that we can be civilized towards each other and seek to exchange and trade what we truly desire. If we agree with the terms of one another's personal boundaries and the rule of law that regulates border control and trade, we can most definitely acquire peace.

Trying to take something that isn't your own culminates into quarrels, fights, or even great civil wars. We have to thus be considerate to respect each other's belongings. We attain peace by realizing that selflessness is the key to wanting those resources in the first place. If we seek to obtain resources from any country or from any state within our country, we have to be mindful of seeking the interests of what our Almighty Creator wants us to do with it. With that consideration, we would never have to fight because we'd then realize that our intentions are pure and divine. Just as our government is controlled by ultimately the divine office, so should our intentions.

The power of intention is one of the greatest driving forces of peace. Our Almighty Creator says it is important to focus on things that are above and not below, to not covet, to be content even in times of hardship or current wealth and success, because when we direct our hearts towards those divine plans we can then be better servants of Allah or our Lord Jesus Christ. There is a difference between wanting or needing, and there is also a difference between asking or taking.

We are all children of our Almighty Creator no matter how tempted we are. It is our onus to make everybody we come in contact with great and revolutionize history for the greater good of all of Humanity.

I am no prophet or some type of guru, but I have a voice, and with this voice, I want to help South Sudan and Sudan my country evolve. I want to thank my country Canada for allowing me to be educated and see the other aspect of life so that I can be aware of worldly affairs so that I can be the change I want to see in the globe.

I also wrote this book so that I can share with all of you the great influence Egypt has had on me by allowing me to understand the purpose of journey. I wanted to show how, in every journey, whether it is towards success or individual or collective peace, it can be possible for a person to appreciate grazing the pastures along the way to a broadened horizon. As for America, you have been the acme of my highest hope and inspiration accomplished. I share the Canadian and American dream by understanding and honoring the great camaraderie and alliance between the two countries.

Epilogue: The Pride Of South Sudan And Sudan – One Country

Since the early eons, the nation of Sudan has fought for its joy, peace, liberty, justice, independence, faith, and harmony. In the duration of this hard-fought civilization, Sudan engineered an unimaginable weaponized cultural phenomenon that would revolutionize its path to reclaim its victory. As a result of the truest form of hope that it can pursue to establish the remarkable pride that uplifts the nation like the immense fuel that launches a rocket. This pride is everlasting because it is embedded in the Sudanese human heart that only knows its transitional channel towards the guiding star.

This wonderful pride maintains the life that isn't in the contour. It purportedly defines the nation or the tribal and religious differences that continue to divide us. However, the magnificence of this pride is unsizable, weightless, and only knows the depth and height for which the Sudanese people choose to plummet and soar. Our pride is also spaceless; that is why it reverberates across the atmosphere like an airless particle. Our pride engages the human heart with unfailing love that knows strife and weakness but redeems itself with the same strength and power that is engaged by the human heart.

Initially, joy is at the very core of all life that exists in our only cherished and beloved country. This is the country that feeds us with the eternal requirement for us to love one another, treat one another with respect, be loyal and committed to the understanding that we are one. It enforces us to belong to the circle of life that we must all share to attain the abundance of milk and honey and the land of cush. Joy also privileges us with the innate contribution that we must make to empower ourselves through our hard work, intelligent work and valuable and principled ethics that we can have in realizing our individual and collective dreams.

Moreover, peace is a never-ending struggle; that doesn't mean we shouldn't strive for it. We must pursue with the lasting patience of what we can to establish it only through trials and tribulations to ossify our bones and reinforce our flesh and ultimately force us to ooze the blood, sweat, equity and tears that formulates us. Peace is reassuring of us that we have not found ourselves but continue the internal and external battle between good and evil to become the newer creation we potentially must become over and over again. Out with the old in with the new, that is the true meaning of peace that liberates us. Just as the cobra scales its skin after a difficult and overbearing journey into the wilderness, the Humanity is subject to the same fate, for we shall battle the elements of human conflict and be reincarnated with a newer belief, character, and reputation.

Similarly, liberty is in the astounding flag that we all must embrace to clear the pathway for us to know and adore our country. To have that newfound freedom that sustains us but also challenges our moral, religious, and educational constraints. So that we may comprehend the real meaning of liberty, that it doesn't just liberates us more and further more, but confines our boundaries so we may finally stretch like the ever-flexible elastic band or leap like the ever risk-taker that is the frog that lives in all of us.

Furthermore, justice is the scale that knows the difference between truth and lies, reality and illusion, black and white that with such indiscriminate continuity it shall always judge conflicts at the heart of the matter. We have to uphold justice not only in the court of law but in the court of life. We can resolve our issues by the common understanding we can have for one another. Because of strands of the peaceful and abundant Sudanese flag we are led towards, it binds and unites us.

However, with reference to independence, it isn't something that we should ever fight for. Whether the land is supposedly colonized or our freedom captured, our history will always remain stable and firm in the knowledge that we are the original citizens and inhabitants. Independence is also like the symbol of a staff that carries our phenomenal flag and waves it with such pride, honor and freedom that it

83

exhibits, to instill in us the valuable and absolute truth. It communicates that no matter the replacement of the flag, it is the staff that is and will always be firmly planted for the purpose of its national existence.

Additionally, faith is what enlivens our vision and enlightens us of our history that we aren't the history itself but the content and the experienced. We must, we will, we can, and we shall have faith in the broadened horizon that exists before and after us. It knows no limit to how far or how short the distance we need to travel to materialize is.

Lastly, harmony is the fulfillment that we need to prolong our history to accept what we can transmute of our human strife and differences. Harmony is also what we need to lend our hands to one another and synchronize our minds to amplify the national, global, and universal intelligence inbred in all of us.

In conclusion, the true pride we should and must have to carry us through sorrow and joy, hatred and love, pain and pleasure, peace and conflict, and harmony and disharmony, is for us to see the opposite and opposing forces all these elements play out. These forces impact us with the tremendous balance that a launching skyrocket is composed of, so that we may direct our efforts towards the guiding star.

Anything is possible!

Our pride engages the human heart with unfailing love that knows strife and weakness, but redeems itself with the same strength and power that is engaged by the human heart.

- Gumaa Lodongi

Citations

Alistair Boddy-Evans. October 24, 2019. Retrieved from https://www.thoughtco.com/john-garang-de-mabior-43576. ThoughtCo.

Lawrence Joffe. June 5 2009. Retrieved from https://www.theguardian.com/world/2009/jun/05/obituary-jaafar-nimeiri. The Guardian.

Your dictionary. Date unknown. Retrieved from https://biography.yourdictionary.com/hassan-abdullah-al-turabi. Your dictionary.

Wikipedia The Free Encyclopedia. January 26 2021. Retrieved from https://en.wikipedia.org/wiki/History_of_Sudan. Wikipedia The Free Encyclopedia.

Kenneth Ingham. Date unknown. Retrieved from https://www.britannica.com/biography/Omar-Hassan-Ahmad-al-Bashir. Britannica.

Amy McKenna. Date unknown. Retrieved from https://www.britannica.com/biography/Salva-Kiir-Mayardit. Britannica.

Author unknown. Date unknown. Retrieved from https://presidency.gov.ss/riakmachar.php.

His Excellency Dr. Riek Machar Teny Dhurgon.

Summary

The Path to Peace: A Never Ending Struggle discusses the valuable ethics concerning the relationship between war and peace. It reveals aspects of life in Sudan before and after it partitioned due to more than several decades of Civil wars and invasion by external countries such as the Arabs, Belgians, British, Anglo-Egyptians, and possibly other unknown nations that settled in Sudan in terms of trades of minerals, and natural resources that Sudan is highly deposited of. Which eventually led to the corruption and enslavement of the Native Sudanese (Nilotics).

This furthermore ignited strife and warring tensions amongst the native tribes of Sudan and there being a civil war between all nations involved in the settlement of Sudan struggling for power, wealth, and dominion over Sudan as a whole and attempting to annihilate the Nilotics over land control and ownership.

The book ends on a positive note stating that "The Path to Peace: A never ending struggle" assures each and every one of us Humanity while we're on earth that through the struggles, tensions, and issues we face that the suffering is what binds our wounds. As we face these struggles again our path towards peace becomes more plausible. Just as our Lord and Savior Jesus Christ bearing the cross of Christ on his way to mount Calvary where he was crucified, died, buried, and rose again. We too, his children, shall experience the same fate by embodying the Christ consciousness and meeting our daily struggles head on and coping with them until we see the beacon of Christ. This Cross of Christ can be a metaphor or literal as long as we possess mercy, love, and compassion until heaven is finalized on earth.

www.ingramcontent.com/pod-product-compliance
Lightning Source LLC
Chambersburg PA
CBHW051034030426
42336CB00015B/2866